in the absence of the sun

emily curtis

ISBN: 0692901264
ISBN-13: 978-0692901267

For Rublee, who told me I could

and Ferry, who told me I should

And here I am, pouring my life into a notebook that will never know its importance.

the nightmares

You didn't listen to me
when I tried to explain
that I have scars so long,
so deep, you may never
find the ends of them

Some people were just designed to be

destructive

When we were younger
we fought with our fists
but now we have discovered
deadlier weapons

-words

Here's to the women who
come home each day,
unbutton the grief, shrug
it off their shoulders and
try to forget it for a while
before they are forced to
wake up and press repeat

Hearts don't shatter
they rot

She's a forest fire,
but she practices self-control

She taught herself to put it out because some people can't
handle incandescence

My biggest fear is that
I will end up telling you
everything that keeps me
up at night

That you will store
this information away
and book a one way flight
while I wait with trembling
hands to see if those files
get leaked

That silly little thing,
she keeps getting herself
into trouble

-my heart

Love, I've found,
is a very selfish beast

What happens under the
blankets can either be

pure magic

or

pure barbarity

and when the latter is reported
it is time and time again mistaken
for the former

-rape culture

We keep white flags
in our back pockets
in case of emergencies

If the pen is mightier than the sword,
my pen is mightier than the
thousands of daggers
you stabbed into my back,
leaving my skin slathered
in blood you so proudly
claim to spill

You scraped the smiles off my face to stich over your permanent scowl, stole my breath so that you could stop holding yours, snatched my eyes to pretend that you were awake, tore off my feet because yours were tired of standing, borrowed my brain so that you could stop hearing the voices that questioned the existence of your own, dug through my skin and cracked my ribs, found my heart and replaced yours in order to finally feel what others felt

The look he gave me through the
dirt-stained windows as he waved me over

The wetness of his face as I entered,
the redness of his cheeks

His swollen eyelids

-the signs

You kiss my cheek and call me pretty
but you and I both know it's only
a matter of time before
we
get
bored

I said "goodnight"
but it sounded more like "goodbye"

That flicker in his eyes,
the one you thought was love,
turned out to be hell and chaos

If he does not respect you now,
he never will

It's impossible to
teach a whale to walk

Lies flow from your lips
thick like molasses
so sweet that
I forget to think twice
before blindly believing
the words you feed me

We are unraveling
like the loose strings
on the sweatshirt
you once gave me

People tend to ignore her
like a crying baby in church

-Truth

The heart-breaker taught me
how to become one

in the absence of the sun

And you just can't seem to fall

                for

                     the

                          prince

You know I am delicate
yet you stand idly by
and watch me
as I wilt

-the daffodil

I sit on the floor
and count my tears
as you vomit words of hate

Little toy girls
playing pretend,
holding back tears
so the powder on
their faces won't
wash away
and reveal
the
truth
beneath
it

You spit lies at my face
while crossing your fingers behind your back
but oh, you fool, you stood in front of a mirror

We
compete
to see
who can
prove
they
    care
        less

He collected us for a living

He had a degree in Lying
and a masters in Manipulation

The shelves are slowly emptying

They are pushed to the corners
to make room for the humming machinery
that comes from this era of novelty

-my room looks more like a library

She told me
she would
barter
her body
for a
prom date
and I
think that
is the
saddest
thing I
have
ever heard

I saw it in his ~~eyes~~ lies

the insomnia

I hope Karma
haunts
your sleep

Slips into
your dreams and
leaves you
sweating and screaming

Things that make me unlovable:

1. the way I twirl my hair out of habit
2. never crying, even when I should
3. getting emotionally attached to books
4. how I use my writing for revenge
5. my quiet competitiveness
6. the way I point out my flaws like I'm trying to convince you of them
7. my constant need to please people
8. my fear of being judged
9. the fact that I made a list of things that makes me unlovable when really the list should only have one number:
10. zero

You are not allowed
to be the main character
of someone else's memoir

It's
12:55 pm
and all that haunts me
are my words
they crawl out
from under my bed
and infest me
they bite
and they screech
and they won't let me be

I keep begging him to stay,
pull up a chair and
have another cup of coffee,
but he always has
somewhere else to be

-Time

The words,
they just
flow out of her
like tears
they dry up
on the pages
and she will
never feel satisfied
because there is
no perfect combination
of letters that will
adequately describe
what she feels

They are all breathing
slower, in sync with
the soft humming of
silence, and I wonder
as their eyelids flutter
who they are dreaming of

I wish I had the
ability to sleep
so peacefully, easily,
but I am among the few
who remain awake
with the owls

-in the absence of the sun

It is strange to think
there was a time
I was unaware of
how much I would
learn to fall in love
with the satisfaction
of spilling my soul
with nothing but a pen
and my words

They compete over who
can become the best
version of generic

I tried my best,
but fixing a human isn't the same as
fixing a bike, or a car

I heard the footsteps of
my fathers steel-toed boots
as he left before the sun had risen
and I thought for a moment
that I took for granted
how hard he works

How dedicated he is

Fatigue dances behind my eyelids,
but my brain still hums
to the melody of the moonlight

It is a monstrous noise

-silence

1 AM and I repeat your name like
it's Sunday, and I am praying for you

Irony: friends sitting together with
screens shoved between their faces
complaining about the weak connection

She was told
so many times
"She can't"
that now
She won't

I leave slowly
one footstep a minute
careful not to wake
the sleeping beast
you have become

Do you know what it feels like
to wait patiently for love
when you know how many
never even receive it?

I do

She looked worn
from a long day in the office
but she did not let one single
complaint slip from her lips as
she turned on the stove to feed
her two nagging kids

-working mother of 2

As I write these words
I ponder how soon I
will forget these words and what
I have to say and why I feel like
writing this and what my pen feels
like scratching away on the notebook
leaning against my legs as I lie here
in silence next to the dog whose name
I will forget 157,680,000 seconds away
from now and by then none of it will
matter

These words I write,
why I decided to write them,
none of it will matter

The love you are selling
has been expired for some time

-discounts won't make it better

She can't help but wonder when
She will be taken under
its wings and taught what
it is like to look down
among the living and
observe quietly

I'm so run down
you can't even tell
what I was before

-road-kill

Who knew mixing
words with feelings
could be so

infuriating

&

intoxicating

I figured if I held my breath long enough and sucked my stomach up under my ribs far enough and powdered my face pale enough and gave myself enough razor burns and plucked the hairs between my eyebrows until my eyes watered and painted my nails girly enough and squeezed my jeans on tight enough and demolished my natural beauty enough I'd be pretty enough

I brave the storm
people call rejection

You fear the damage they
could do if you let them
know your secrets

-why you push them away

emily curtis

I live among the hardcovers
stacked in piles higher than Everest
because it is easier to feel
through fictional characters
the loss
the love
the heartbreak
the tragedy
it all comes at once
and then it is gone
with the close of the cover

-from the comfort of my bedroom

Not quite sure if this is love or just me
pretending he is something I should have

            up
        up
up

where the tears
flow, a fresh stream
of saltwater

down
        down
                down
                        down

where your darkest days
reside, the place in which
you feel the end is near,
a quick jerk to the left
and you have reached the
residence of your old
friend Denial, she is kind
to you, asks you to stay
for a while, but you are
launched to the right and

            up
        up
up

again to where days are
spent mopping pools of
saltwater that once
dripped from your eyelashes
like oil from a wrecked car,
a home for the words

"okay"

&

"fine"

&

"I'll get through this"

then it evens out, parallel
with the horizon and the
engine loses life, the
ride is now over, please
exit to your left and pick up
all of your belongings, have a
nice day and try never to visit again

-the emotional rollercoaster

To cry over spilled milk is completely acceptable

-the tears will not end you

in the absence of the sun

the dreams

They say freedom is expressed through goodbyes

"Goodbye," I say, "Goodbye!"

in the absence of the sun

One word
is all it takes
to erase the word
"Stranger"

-hello

There will always be
a loose screw
or an uneven floorboard

-there is no such thing as a perfect life

I need
my old friend
Patience
to stop by and
remind me to
wait and blindly trust
with more grace

Why are we constantly
told we know nothing of it?
it isn't something
we grow into
[like our bodies]
it is something
we have the capability
of feeling as soon as
we hear our mothers laugh,
or our fathers say our name

Life leads rivers for those willing to follow
with a paddle and a fishing net

Empathy tugs lightly
on my shirt sleeve
and gently whispers in my ear,
"they are struggling too"

"Oh what a pity
they cannot witness
the beauty of a sunrise
while parallel to it"

-what the birds say when they sing

You're not out of my league,
there are no leagues

-we're all equal here

We forget the beauty in the trees
as their leaves turn the color of sunshine

-04967

What do I know of love?

Nothing.

"Teach me," I begged him,
"Teach me"

You have woken me up
and convinced me
that love is not
                    [Pointless]
                    [Impossible]
                    [Dead]
                    [Worthless]

Falling for you
was like rereading
my favorite book

You are ~~allowed~~ encouraged to be different

You tear me down like
last year's calendar on New Year's Day

My resolution is to stop letting you

She tells a story with each stroke of paint,
and creates masterpieces with her words

-the poet with a paintbrush

It is a constant reminder
to ignore the bloodshed
that spreads like the plague,
the gloom that seeps
through the ceilings,
the disappointment that
sleeps at the foot of
your bed

-sunlight

You've got me hooked,
like how any good author
grabs the attention of an
enthusiastic reader
you know how to use those first
few words to your advantage

You act like I need you
to survive but I don't

I have plenty of oxygen, thanks

And I never used to speak out of turn,
the latch on my mouth remained untouched,
but that changed sometime in between the

"you can'ts"

&

"you don't dare's"

Her death was not Her end

And right after your ABC's
you learn that
God created everyone equal,
pink is not just a girl's color,
and boys are allowed to cry

-how it should be

We are splatter paint on a blank canvas

s-c-a-t-t-e-r-e-d

spoNtaNeOus

unapologetically messy

All the daisies, violets,
daffodils, roses, orchids,
tulips, sunflowers, carnations,
lilies, chrysanthemums, peonies,
amaryllis, baby's breath, calla,
delphiniums, gardenias, heathers,
hydrangeas, irises, Queen Anne's lace,
snapdragons, azaleas, begonias,
bluebells, buttercups, camellias,
dahlias, daylilies, forget-me-nots
or primroses, even geraniums or
gladioluses, hibiscus or hostas,
lavender or lilacs' wouldn't
convince me to take you back

so please, don't waste your money

You're my prince charming
but I'm not your princess

I dream of you in my sleep
but you've already fought a dragon
for her

Thank you for being my armor

even on the days when my battle cry was
"it's impossible"

He had second thoughts because
I didn't own a tiara
I didn't wear gowns
I wore ripped jeans and kicks
I slurped my soup
and let my hair hang
loosely, wildly off my shoulders
I wasn't a damsel in distress
and didn't *need* a prince
to sweep me off my feet

You can't see it
it's not something
you can hold
in your hand
but you feel it
when he touches you
you hear it in the
deep breaths after
long kisses
you taste it on his lips
you know it's there
more than anything
you have ever known
and you know that
it will never leave

Learn to take a complement with grace

even if you don't believe it

And then I see the fallen ones
and it makes me wonder if they
were knocked down or if
they didn't have the strength
to stay rooted to the ground

-I understand now that some roots are just too weak

Reality smokes about a thousand packs of them a day,
never pausing to consider what opportunities he would
have if he quit, what the world would become if he wasn't
addicted to lighting them up only to inhale one puff and
then stub them out, reaching for another to waste because
each new one is more fresh than the last

-our dreams

I want to hear
your voice
I want to hear
the melodies of
your demise, how your
sound flickers through
the air
like a gentle flame
so mesmerizing
I pray that it will
never be put out

-sing like the birds

emily curtis

in the absence of the sun

emily curtis

Acknowledgements

I.   My parents, who are always encouraging. To put
        it simply, thank you for believing in me.

II.   My aunt and uncle, for all the help getting here
        (literally) in the first place.

III.   The rest of my small but loving family, who I
        know will read this and wonder where it all
        came from.

IV.   My editors and peers, for the opinions and
        support I needed to share it all.

V.   Again, Rublee and Ferry, who told me it was
        possible even when I was certain it wasn't.

emily curtis

About the Author

Emily Curtis is a poet from Maine who you can always find with a book one in hand and a cup of tea in the other. She is a lover of poetry, music, art, animals, the beach, and above all, friends and family. She currently attends Foxcroft Academy, in Dover-Foxcroft, Maine, and receives support from many of her peers and teachers there. This is her first poetry collection and hopefully not her last. As for her future, it is still unclear, but one thing is for certain: writing will be a part of it. You can find her on Instagram as *@poetryflowssofter*.

emily curtis